Wolfgang Ecke (1927–1983)

Sein Name ist zu einem Begriff für gute, spannende Unterhaltung geworden. Seine Bücher beziehen ihre Spannung aus der Aufforderung zum Mitdenken, durch lebendige, oft humorvolle Dialoge – und nicht durch sensationelle Gewalt. Wolfgang Ecke sagte selbst: »Ich behaupte, es gibt keinen Kinder-Krimi! Es gibt nur Kriminalgeschichten, die als Lektüre für Kinder geeignet sind; wobei es unbedeutend ist, ob sie eigens für Kinder geschrieben wurden.«

Er hat über 600 Hörspiele geschrieben, von denen unzählige, ebenso wie ein Großteil seiner über fünfzig Bücher, in viele Sprachen übersetzt wurden. Er war ständiger Mitarbeiter bei zahlreichen in- und ausländischen Radiosendern, schrieb für Jugendzeitschriften, produzierte Platten und auch einige Fernsehfilme. In den Ravensburger Taschenbüchern sind neben mehreren Einzeltiteln folgende Serien von ihm erschienen:

Wer knackt die Nuß?
Perry Clifton
Club der Detektive (auch auf englisch und französisch)
Tom Knall und die Libelle
Meisterdetektiv Balduin Pfiff
Wolfgang Eckes Kriminalmagazin

Für mehr als vier Millionen verkaufte Ravensburger Taschenbücher erhielt Ecke viermal das »Goldene Taschenbuch«.

Wolfgang Ecke selbst über sein Leben:

»Geboren dort, wo Karl May starb: in Radebeul, und zwar am 24. November 1927. Schulbesuch, da Pflicht. ›Sehr gut‹ in Deutsch und Geographie. Alle übrigen Zensuren nicht überlieferungswürdig. Mit 13 Jahren in ein militärisches Internat. Außer Marschieren und Strammstehen auch Klavier, Schlagzeug und Fagott gelernt. Gelungener Versuch, den Krieg unbeschadet zu überleben. Danach Hochschule für Musik und Theater in Dresden. Bereits 1946 aus politischen Gründen von der Hochschule relegiert.«
Zwischen 1945 und 1952 lebte Ecke »abwechselnd überall und in Dresden«. Anfang der 70er Jahre ließ er sich mit seiner Frau und seinen beiden Töchtern (und zwei afghanischen Windhunden und zahlreichen Katzen) im bayerischen Alpenvorland nieder; zuletzt wohnte er oberhalb des Staffelsees in Murnau.

Wolfgang Ecke

The Face
at the Window

and other detective stories

Otto Maier Verlag Ravensburg

Hinweis

Schwierige Vokabeln werden nur beim ersten Auftreten in den Fußnoten unten auf der Seite aufgeführt, ansonsten im alphabetischen Gesamtverzeichnis. Andere Vokabeln sind nur im alphabetischen Gesamtverzeichnis am Schluß des Buches zu finden. Es empfiehlt sich also, häufiger dort nachzuschlagen.

Erstmals 1979 in den Ravensburger Taschenbüchern
© 1971 und 1972 Otto Maier Verlag Ravensburg
English translation copyright © 1978
Methuen Children's Books Ltd., London
Titel der englischen Ausgabe:
"Be A Super Sleuth with the Case of the Face at the Window"

Englische Übersetzung: Stella und Vernon Humphries
Die Geschichten sind erstmals in folgenden
Ravensburger Taschenbüchern auf deutsch erschienen:
Band 208 Das Schloß der roten Affen
Band 214 Der Mann in Schwarz
Band 221 Das Gesicht an der Scheibe
Bearbeitung: Uwe Lüer

Illustrationen: Rolf Rettich
Umschlaggestaltung: Graphisches Atelier Otto Maier Verlag,
unter Verwendung einer Zeichnung von Rolf Rettich

Alle Rechte dieser Ausgabe vorbehalten durch
Otto Maier Verlag Ravensburg
Druck und Verarbeitung: Ebner Ulm

5   83

ISBN 3-473-39560-9

Contents

Solutions: *easy
           **quite difficult
         ***difficult

1 The face at the window

Paul Daimler looked thoughtfully at the letter in his hand. He wasn't sure what to do. Should he post it, or should he tear it up?

Wouldn't it make his nephew Frank believe that Paul was becoming rather odd now that he was growing old, that he had started seeing things that weren't there? Once more he read through what he had written:

Dear Frank,

You know you are the only relation I have, the only person I can write to. I'm hoping you can help me. There are strange things going on here, and I would have gone to the police a long time ago if I hadn't been afraid they'd laugh at me. And it's no laughing matter from my point of view, I can tell you. I do hope you at least will take me seriously. As I've already said, the whole business is most peculiar.

It's about four weeks now since it all started.

One evening, I was sitting on the couch in the living-room, listening to the radio. Suddenly, outside, I saw a man's face pressed against the win-

thoughtful(ly)	– gedankenvoll
to post	– zur Post geben, abschicken
odd	– komisch, sonderbar
nephew	– Neffe
relation	– Verwandter
peculiar	– seltsam

dow. At first it gave me such a shock I couldn't even move. I swear it wasn't a ghost, but a living person, who stared at me and then pulled a hideous face. I quickly got a torch and went out into the garden, but he had disappeared.

The same thing happened again during the next few days, no less than five times. Sometimes he tapped at the window as well, and every time,

when I turned to look, this hideous face pressed itself against the glass.

From time to time he left me alone and then, the day before yesterday, something even stranger happened. I was out shopping when I actually saw the man in person. He was in one of the big stores, making a telephone call, and I knew him by his face at once. I could even hear his name. He was saying: "This is Walters speaking." I hadn't the courage to go up to him, but when he caught sight of me he actually raised his hat and called "Good morning!" What does this fellow Walters want of me? I don't know him nor anyone else called Walters. And last night he was there again, at the window. I went straight upstairs to bed. What ought I to do, Frank. Can't you help me?

Your loving uncle,

Paul

Paul Daimler nodded to himself. Yes, he had described exactly what had happened, no more, no less. So he sealed the envelope and took it to the letterbox. On the way, he twice caught himself turning round nervously in case somebody followed him.

Then Paul Daimler began to wait for an answer. A week passed, then another. And he might well

hideous	– gräßlich
to tap	– pochen
actually	– tatsächlich
to describe	– beschreiben
to seal	– zukleben
in case	– falls

have waited a third week, if there had not been that particular Sunday…

It had all started peacefully enough. After church he went to lunch at Robert Lesser's house. Lesser, who used to work in the same office before Daimler retired, invited him to lunch regularly once a month. As Lesser said, the lonely widower should get a really good meal at least once in four weeks. After lunch the two men played chess for about four hours, and after sitting still for so long they had gone for a long walk. It was therefore shortly before eight o'clock that evening that Daimler arrived home.

There was a good film on television in half an hour, so Paul decided he would watch it and go to bed straight after the late news. Then once again…

By now it was ten minutes to eleven, and the weather-map for the following day had just been shown on the screen. Paul Daimler happened to turn his head. The face! The face was there again, as always, with lips and nose hard against the glass and twisted into a grimace. Daimler stared at it, hypnotized. He wanted to get to his feet, but his legs wouldn't move. Suddenly the face disappeared…

It took quite some time before the old man recov-

---

particular	– besondere(r)
to retire	– in Pension gehen
chess	– Schach
to twist	– verzerren, verdrehen
grimace	– Grimasse
to recover	– wiedergewinnen

ered his self-possession. Had there been a telephone in the house, he would certainly have rung the police this time.

With tired legs and heavy arms, he dragged himself upstairs to bed and during a sleepless night he made up his mind. He wouldn't wait any longer for Frank's answer to his letter. Instead he would go and see him. It was no use putting it off any longer. He would go next day.

It was already dark when the train pulled in at Breitenberg station, so Paul Daimler took a taxi. But even before the driver had crossed the square in front of the station, the old man felt anxious. Suppose his nephew was away from home? What would he do then?

It was a great relief when he came to Frank's house and saw that he was in. There was a light burning in his flat.

He paid the taxi driver and rang the bell.

Frank Daimler was an insurance agent of about thirty. "It can't be true!" he exclaimed in astonishment. "My Uncle Paul has come all this way to see me!"

Paul Daimler hugged his nephew happily and arm

self-possession	— Selbstbeherrschung
to make up one's mind	— einen Entschluß fassen
to put off	— verschieben
to suppose	— annehmen; hier: angenommen
relief	— Erleichterung
flat	— Wohnung
insurance agent	— Versicherungsvertreter
to hug	— umarmen

in arm they entered Frank's bachelor flat.

"This is such a surprise, Uncle Paul. When the bell rang, you were the last person I expected to see. I wondered who on earth it might be. I never dreamed it might be you."

Paul Daimler sat down heavily in an armchair. "If only you'd answered my letter I'd never have inflicted myself on you," he replied.

Franks face showed great astonishment. "A letter? What letter?"

This time it was Daimler's turn to look surprised. "The one I wrote to you, of course."

"When?"

"A good two weeks ago."

"I haven't received any letter from you."

The old man couldn't believe that. "Are you certain?" he asked.

"A hundred per cent. I've been at home for the last four weeks, and I've picked up the post myself every day. But don't look so worried. Now that you're here in person, you can tell me everything face to face instead. Would you like something to eat or drink?"

"I wouldn't say no to a glass of beer – that is, if you have any."

Frank sprang to his feet. "Of course there's beer. I'll go and fetch it."

When Frank had poured out a glass of beer for his

---

bachelor	– Junggeselle
to inflict on someone	– sich jemandem aufdrängen

uncle he came straight to the point. "Come on, now. Tell me what's the trouble."

The old gentleman gave his nephew a long serious look before replying. "Frank, do you take me for an old fool who's suddenly started seeing things?"

First surprise, then amusement passed over the young man's face. He looked at his uncle quizzically and grinned. "And I really thought it was something serious," he laughed.

"My question was perfectly serious, Frank," answered Paul curtly.

"I thought you were pulling my leg," said Frank defensively.

"I'd hardly have made such a long journey just for a practical joke."

Frank tried to calm him down. "All right, Uncle Paul. I certainly don't consider you an old fool who's suddenly seeing things. Suppose you tell me what it's all about?"

For a while the old man sat still, as if lost in thought. Then he spoke. "For several weeks now I've been seeing the same face, again and again, pressed against the window. Sometimes it's in the kitchen, sometimes in the living-room. Sometimes it taps on the glass…"

---

to come straight to the point	– sogleich zur Hauptsache kommen
quizzical(ly)	– seltsam; spöttisch
curt(ly)	– kurz, bestimmt
defensively	– verteidigend
practical joke	– Streich, Schabernack
to calm down	– beruhigen
to consider	– ansehen als

"What kind of face is it?" Frank's voice showed his interest and he watched his uncle closely.

"It's a man's face, Frank, a man's face that contorts itself into the most hideous expressions. For weeks now he's been coming almost every day, and it worries me so much that I can't think of anything else. Why does he do it?"

His nephew leaned forward. His voice sounded really sympathetic as he asked: "Wouldn't you like a brandy, Uncle?" And he jumped back, almost in alarm, when the old man shouted: "I knew all along you'd think I'm crazy!"

"No, no, Uncle Paul," said Frank. "Nothing of the sort. Come on, now. Tell me the rest of the story."

Daimler made an angry gesture. "What else is there to tell? I've even seen the fellow in a shop. He raised his hat politely and said 'Good morning!'"

"And why don't you go to the police?"

"They'd never believe me."

"But you don't know they won't if you don't try."

"I don't want to hear them saying that I'm not right in the head. And they'd hardly send a policeman to come to the house and keep watch all day and night, waiting for the face to appear, now

to contort	– verziehen
expression	– (Gesichts-)Zug, Ausdruck
to lean forward	– sich vorbeugen
sympathetic	– mitfühlend
crazy	– verrückt
gesture	– Geste
to keep watch	– Wache halten

would they?"

"All the same, I'd report it if I were you. The police ought to arrest this fellow Walters. Isn't that why we pay taxes? So the police have a duty to do something for us. I for one have to work jolly hard to earn my money, and I have to show results, too!"

Paul Daimler listened carefully. "That's all very well," he answered. "But suppose this Walters turns out to be a most respectable citizen, with witnesses to swear he's the kindest, most decent man in the world? What a fool I'd look!"

For a while there was silence. Then Frank said: "Do go and see the doctor, Uncle. Perhaps there really is something wrong with your nerves. After all, you're alone in the house all day, talking to yourself... Why don't you sell the house and move into a flat? Or you could let the place..."

Paul Daimler's face showed how disappointed he was in his nephew. And his voice sounded sad as he said: "I'm tired, Frank. I think it's time for bed."

---

to report	– melden
taxes	– Steuern
I for one	– ich zum Beispiel
result	– Ergebnis, Resultat
to turn out	– sich herausstellen
citizen	– Bürger
witness	– Zeuge
to swear	– schwören
decent	– anständig
to let	– vermieten
to persuade	– überreden

Next morning, Frank could not persuade the old man to stay for a few days longer. And as he got into the train Paul Daimler was sure that his only relation considered him a silly old man whose imagination was running away with him and who thought he was seeing ghosts.

He had no idea that he was quite mistaken in this, that the truth in fact was different – and much nastier: that his own nephew Frank was having a hand in the affair, that Frank was paying the "face at the window" to haunt his uncle.

Why was Frank doing it? That must remain his secret. He may have had an eye on his uncle's little house. Who knows?

What was the mistake Frank Daimler made? With what remark did he betray that he knew more about the man at the window than he was ready to admit?

---

imagination	– Fantasie
to run away with	– durchgehen
to be mistaken	– im Irrtum sein, sich täuschen
nasty	– unangenehm
to haunt	– verfolgen
remark	– Bemerkung

2 The fare-dodger

At a constant high speed, the night express from
Amsterdam to Cologne raced along the track.
There was something eerie about the lighted win-
dows and flickering streetlamps which were slip-
ping silently past.
The time was 23.15.
Hilversum and Utrecht were already far behind
and the train rushed on, through Doorn station.
Most of the passengers were either reading or
asleep, and only a few peered through the win-
dows.
A man in an olive-green trenchcoat was working
his way along the corridor of a first-class coach.
But every now and then he looked furtively over
his shoulder to make sure no one was watching
him.
He had a short look into each compartment, and
at last he appeared to have found the one he
wanted. Near the window, the two men facing
each other in the corner seats seemed to be sleep-

dodger	– Schwindler
track	– Strecke
eerie	– unheimlich
to flicker	– flackern
coach	– Wagen
to peer	– gucken
furtive(ly)	– verstohlen
compartment	– Abteil

ing soundly. Two of the other seats must also have been taken: a pair of gloves was on one of them and a book on the other; neither passenger was there at that moment.

The new arrival took off his coat, quietly placed his suitcase in the rack, and sat down beside one of the sleeping passengers, whose gentle rhythmic snoring continued undisturbed, even when some fin-

sound(ly)	–	tief
gloves	–	Handschuhe
rack	–	(Koffer-)Ablage
snoring	–	Schnarchen
undisturbed	–	ungestört

gers touched his suit. As soon as the stranger had found what he was looking for, he immediately switched to another seat. And none too soon either, for just then the other two men returned to the compartment. They nodded, sat down and didn't take any further notice of the others.

The silence was suddenly broken. "Tickets please!" called a voice.

The two sleepers were at once awake and five hands dived into their pockets.

The guard had already checked and returned four of the tickets when he turned to the gentleman on seat number seventy, who was still fumbling in his pockets and becoming very nervous. "Don't you worry, sir," said the guard quietly. "Just go on looking for your ticket and I'll come back later." With a friendly smile he left the compartment and went on his way to the next one.

"Perhaps you left it in your overcoat pocket," suggested the passenger in seat number seventy-one opposite.

"No, no. That's impossible. I know I had it here in my jacket."

"You could be mistaken," murmured number seventy-one, and number seventy-three also tried to be helpful: "It's so easy to pull out a ticket by

---

to switch to	– hinüberrutschen, wechseln
none too soon	– keinen Augenblick zu früh
further	– weitere
to check	– überprüfen
guard	– Schaffner

mistake when you go to your pocket for something else. I've often done it myself."

Again and again the unfortunate man searched all his pockets. "I can't believe it," he said, "I'm sure I had it here." And he patted the pocket on his right side. "Didn't any of you gentlemen notice it, on the floor perhaps?"

"Sorry," said number seventy-three with a shrug. "I only got in at Doorn."

And also the traveller in seat number seventy-one could only tell how sorry he was. "I can't help either, I'm afraid. I fell asleep soon after we left Amsterdam. What about you?" he asked, turning to seat number sixty-eight.

"I've been in the dining-car most of the time. …But don't I remember seeing you with a newspaper in that pocket when we started our journey? Or am I mistaken?"

The man in the corner seat denied this angrily. "Nothing of the sort," he replied. "I didn't even buy an evening paper today. In fact, I forgot."

The man in number sixty-nine raised his eyebrows sceptically. "Maybe you have forgotten to buy a ticket as well?"

For a moment it looked as if number seventy was going to give his neighbour a punch in his face.

---

to pat	– klopfen (auf)
to deny	– zurückweisen
to raise	– erheben
punch	– Schlag, Stoß

Then he thought better of it and confined himself to an angry gesture. Five minutes later he resigned and sighed: "It's simply disappeared into thin air. I suppose I'll have to pay again. There's nothing else I can do."

The guard, too, came to the same conclusion when, a short time later, he came back to the compartment. Grinding his teeth angrily, the man in seat number seventy handed over the required sum. His fellow passengers looked at him with disapproval, even contempt. No one has any sympathy with fare-dodgers.

In which seat was the real fare-dodger sitting?

to confine	– sich beschränken
to resign	– resignieren
required	– benötigt(e)
to grind	– knirschen
disapproval	– Mißbilligung
contempt	– Verachtung

3 Find the mistakes

What do you think? Would you be clever enough to work as a detective? There are a number of mistakes in this story: see how many you can find!
In the great entrance hall hung two fine oil-paintings, portraits of the famous Americans, Charles Dickens, who was once President of the United States, and the well-known novelist Abraham Lincoln.
The hall was full of people, and Inspector Mulligan of Scotland Yard reckoned that the number of those who had come that evening to celebrate the fiftieth birthday of Sir Arthur Hull, must be at least a hundred. It was the duty of Mulligan and his three junior police officers to keep an eye on things. They had to ensure that nothing unpleasant happened to the guests, who included some of the most important people in the country. He was particularly worried, because there had been an anonymous telephone call earlier in the day, say-

entrance hall	– Eingangshalle
oil painting	– Ölgemälde
novelist	– (Roman-)Schriftsteller
to reckon	– schätzen, rechnen
to celebrate	– feiern
duty	– Aufgabe, Pflicht
to ensure	– sicherstellen
unpleasant	– unangenehm
to include	– einschließen
particularly	– besonders

22

ing that a notorious pickpocket might well turn up and try to mingle with the people.

As soon as Mulligan was informed that all the invited guests had arrived, he called his men together and went over his instructions very precisely. "I'm relying on you to keep your eyes open," he stressed. "The downstairs rooms open on to terraces on all four sides of the house, and the double doors leading to these terraces are the most likely danger points. Try to behave naturally and make yourselves as inconspicuous as possible. Is everything clear now? Good. Then let's go. I want you, Black, to take the north door. Ross will keep an eye on the south side. Forrester, will you guard the west, please, and Pullman, will you make sure no one tries any nonsense near the east door? Any questions? No? Then take up your positions."

At that moment there was a fanfare from the eight-piece orchestra, and a gentleman in dark blue dinner jacket stepped on the stage. In his right hand he held a glass of champagne. "Ladies and gentlemen!" he began. "I know I'm speaking for everyone here if I now raise my glass and ask you to join me in drinking the health of our ex-

pickpocket	– Taschendieb
to turn up	– auftauchen
to mingle	– sich mischen (unter)
to rely on	– sich verlassen auf
to behave	– sich benehmen, verhalten
inconspicuous	– unauffällig
eight-piece~	– Acht-Mann~
to drink the health	– auf die Gesundheit trinken

cellent host, Sir Arthur. We all wish him well in his new office, and congratulate him heartily on his appointment as a minister in Her Majesty's government."

There was a storm of applause, everyone drank Sir Arthur's health and sang "For he's a jolly good fellow". Then there were a few speeches and the evening's entertainment began.

Inspector Mulligan kept watching the guests. Who was the pickpocket and what was his disguise? How the inspector wished the anonymous letter had been nothing but a practical joke!

It was about ten o'clock that the cabaret started. At first a conjurer appeared. He started by asking if twelve of the gentlemen would lend him their gold pocket-watches. These he placed in his top hat. He then climbed on a chair, lifted one hand as if to give a signal, and all the lights went out. For a few seconds there was an anxious silence.

When the lights went on again an astonished murmur showed that the people had indeed been taken by surprise, and Inspector Mulligan broke

host	– Gastgeber
to congratulate	– gratulieren
appointment	– Ernennung
government	– Regierung
speech	– Rede
entertainment	– Unterhaltung
disguise	– Verkleidung
conjurer	– Zauberer
top hat	– Zylinder
silence	– Schweigen
murmur	– Murmeln
to be taken by surprise	– in Erstaunen versetzt werden

25

into a cold sweat. For the conjurer had disappeared, and in his place a beautiful ballet dancer was balancing gracefully on the chair. This young lady waved her arms and danced until the lights went out a second time. The audience held its breath. And after ten seconds, the four chandeliers blazed into light once more and on the chair stood – the conjurer!

He held his top hat high up and – turned it upside down! It was empty.

"Gentlemen, please," he called above the murmur, "will you be good enough to look and see if all your watches are back in position?" Automatically the fingers of the eleven men dived into their pockets. Yes, all the watches had been safely returned. There was thunderous applause.

The party was a great success. And when Inspector Mulligan and his men left the house at four o'clock the following morning, he was very pleased and enormously relieved. Nothing, but nothing, had been stolen.

Can you find the mistakes in this story? How many are there?

---

gracefully	– graziös
breath	– Atem
chandelier	– Kronleuchter
to blaze into light	– hell aufleuchten
in position	– an Ort und Stelle
to return	– hier: zurückgeben
thunderous	– donnernd
to relieve	– erleichtern

4 A case for Interpol

The man with the cold black eyes and the pencil-thin moustache crossed the tavern looking straight ahead. At the bar he stopped and asked: "Is the Chief in?"

The old man behind the bar nodded just a bit, and a key changed hands.

Without so much as a "Thank you" the new arrival walked straight to the washroom. One of the three doors inside was inscribed *private*, and it was this one that the key fitted. Behind it stretched a long corridor that ended in stairs.

Taking these stairs two at a time, the man seemed at first to take no notice of the large oil-paintings on each side. But at the top he paused in front of one picture. With his hand he touched the canvas, tapping out a short rhythm, and all at once the painting began to turn like a door.

The man stepped forward. Immediately the paint-

moustache	– Schnurrbart
tavern	– Taverne, Schenke
straight ahead	– geradeaus
arrival	– Ankömmling
inscribed	– mit der Inschrift versehen
to fit	– passen zu
to take notice	– Notiz nehmen, beachten
canvas	– Leinwand
to tap	– klopfen
rhythm	– Rhythmus

ing closed soundlessly behind him.

He was in a large room, full of cupboards, bookshelves and a number of leather armchairs. On the walls hung large maps of all the continents, and the floor was covered with wonderful carpets and rugs.

At a huge paper-covered desk a man with a deeply tanned face and snow-white hair was sitting. "Back from Ankara already? I didn't expect you till tomorrow at the earliest." His voice was deep, with a metallic ring to it.

The other man dropped into a deep leather armchair. "It went much more quickly than we thought possible, Chief. The next consignment is ready."

"What about the quality?"

"Excellent. There's only one thing I'm not happy about. I think Patani is getting… well… let's say nervous."

The white-haired man put down his gold pen and gave his visitor a searching look. "What do you mean. How is he nervous? Has something happened?" His voice sounded ominous.

"He believes there are signs that Interpol has been

---

soundless	– lautlos
leather	– Leder
to cover	– bedecken
rug	– (Teppich-)Brücke
tanned	– gebräunt
ring	– Beiklang
consignment	– Lieferung
to give a searching look	– forschend anblicken
ominous	– unheilvoll

tipped off. One of his men was picked up in Izmir last week."

"Any stuff on him?"

"No. Only a forged passport. But Patani thinks we ought to send the next goods via Aksarai on the twenty-third. If we agree, Dogan can switch the package at the ruins. The method as before... the one we can trust."

The man at the desk leaned back to look at a wall-map of Europe. His eyes seemed to be drawn to one particular spot. Almost a minute passed before either spoke. Then the white-haired man sat forward again. "How much is Patani delivering this time?" he asked.

"Seven hundred thousand in one hundred dollar notes."

"Good. Ring Dogan and tell him."

Without another word the visitor rose from his chair and picked up the telephone on the desk. With the gold pen he dialled. The ringing tone at the other end could be heard clearly, and then a voice said: "Dogan speaking."

"Hello, Dogan. Ismet here. The new consignment will go via Aksarai this time on the twenty-third. The ususal package switch. Using Number Three

to tip someone off	– jemand einen Tip geben, warnen
to pick up	– erwischen, schnappen
stuff	– Stoff, hier: Falschgeld
forged	– gefälscht
to switch	– austauschen, übergeben
to dial	– wählen
package switch	– Gepäcktausch

type packaging. The ten to twelve conducted tour. End of message."

When the man who called himself Ismet had put the receiver down the Chief called in a tone of command: "And now get me Patani!"

All this happened on Friday the sixteenth. It was one of the hot days in Istanbul, the largest city in Turkey, that made breathing difficult even for someone lying still. Not a bit of air came in from the Bosporus to bring a touch of coolness.

One of those who usually suffered in such weather was Miss Joanna Minetti, a special correspondent for a number of West European newspapers. But that Friday afternoon the lady journalist forgot all about the heat. What had happened was so re-markable that she jumped into her car and drove as fast as she could to the city centre, where she arrived shortly after four o'clock.

At ten minutes past four, she was shown into a room where there were two men. To her surprise, they were both in plain clothes and not in uniform. As she entered, they rose politely and the elder of the two spoke first.

---

conducted tour	– Reise mit (Fremden-)Führung
message	– Mitteilung
receiver	– Telefonhörer
breathing	– Atmen
touch of coolness	– ein wenig Kühle
to suffer in	– leiden unter
remarkable	– bemerkenswert
in plain clothes	– hier: in Zivil
politely	– höflich

"Good afternoon, Miss. I'm Chief Inspector Kolai, and this is my colleague, Inspector Kemal. You wanted a word with me, I believe."

The lady nodded. "Yes, I'm Joanna Minetti…" she introduced herself. "You see, I'm a journalist working here in Istanbul. Generally I do my work quite independently, and if I do not in this particular case it's because I'm afraid it may be too big to tackle by myself… and it's probably too 'hot' as well."

She paused a moment and when next she spoke she stressed every word carefully. "But if you, the police, take action, I want to be present. That's why I said I'm a journalist."

The two men looked at each other amused. Then Kolai spoke. "I must admit you've certainly made us curious. What's it all about, Miss Minetti?"

"First I must ask you a question. Have you got a tape-recorder here in the office?"

Kolai nodded and crossed the room to a cupboard, which was full of all kinds of equipment. "Here we are," he said, putting a tape-recorder on the table.

Miss Joanna Minetti handed a tape to the officer. "When I'm going to be out," she explained, "I fix

to introduce oneself	– sich vorstellen
independently	– unabhängig
particular case	– besonderer Fall
to tackle	– schaffen, fertig werden mit
to take action	– in Aktion treten
to admit	– zugeben
what's it all about?	– worum geht es nun eigentlich?
equipment	– Gerät
to fix	– anschließen

an answering machine to my telephone to record incoming calls for me. But this one has nothing at all to do with me, and I've no idea how it came on the tape. So it's no use asking me. I can't even begin to guess what it's about. Will you play it now please."

Chief Inspector Kolai placed the type on the machine. "Very well then. Surprise us!" he said cheerfully, and pressed the playback key.

A short burst of atmospherics filled the room, followed by a whistle and finally a voice: "...gan speaking."

"Hello, Dogan. Ismet here. The new consignment will go via Aksarai this time on the twenty-third. The usual package switch. Using Number Three type packaging. The ten to twelve conducted tour..."

Immediately after the word "tour" the shrill whistle returned and Kolai switched off.

Both police officers looked very serious all at once, and their change of expression was not lost on Miss Minetti, who felt herself going hot and cold. But she put on a brave face and in a voice as normal as possible she asked: "Well, Chief Inspector? Is it 'hot' or isn't it?"

Kolai's voice was as serious as his face. "If I were

---

answering machine	– Telefonbeantworter
to record	– aufzeichnen
playback key	– Wiedergabetaste
burst of atmospherics	– Schwall von atmosphärischen Störungen
was not lost on...	– verfehlte seine Wirkung nicht auf...

superstitious, I'd perhaps say it was Fate, or Kismet as they call it in the Moslem world. But let's just agree that it's a remarkable coincidence. You see, Miss Minetti, Inspector Kemal is from the Interpol Bureau in Ankara. And the information you have just given us fits in with what we were discussing like the missing piece of a puzzle." Here he turned to Inspector Kemal, inviting him to speak. "Please, Kemal, explain to Miss Minetti what it's all about."

"With pleasure!" said Kemal. "For the past few months, we've been after a gang who are printing forged American dollar notes. Until now we've had little success. It's true we've picked up one or two of their small fish from time to time. We have an idea, too, that a certain Achmed Patani has a finger in the pie... But that isn't enough. We're looking for the brains behind the organization."

"And you're sure this telephone call has something to do with these forgeries?"

"I'm not certain, but I very much hope so. A few weeks ago, we arrested one of Patani's friends, and that's why they operate as far away as Aksarai."

"Where is Aksarai? Isn't it a place where there are

superstitious	– abergläubisch
fate	– Schicksal
coincidence	– Zufall, Zusammentreffen
to fit in	– hineinpassen
pleasure	– Vergnügen
finger in the pie	– die Hand im Spiel
brains	– führende Köpfe
to operate	– hier: Geschäfte abwickeln

some famous historic ruins?"

Kemal nodded. "That's right. It's half way between Kayseri and Konya."

At this point, Chief Inspector Kolai again joined in the discussion. "In fact, you can be sure that the so-called package switch will take place among the ruins."

"That'll be it!" Kemal agreed emphatically. "I don't know of any other place in that region where there are conducted tours. The only difficulty so far is that there are three tourist attractions in the area: the Gayana Tower, the Romchiko Caves, and the Cersa Rocks... We'll have to seal off all three places."

Joanna Minetti listened. "What happens on these tours?" she asked.

"From time to time a minibus arrives at a certain stop to set down visitors and to pick up those who've finished their sightseeing. That is where we must be, ready and waiting."

Miss Minetti nodded. Then, in a voice that refused to take 'no' for an answer, she said firmly: "Then I'll keep the twenty-third free."

The Chief Inspector grinned. "I think we could object strongly, but if you really want to, we'll not

---

to join in	– sich beteiligen
emphatically	– voller Überzeugung
caves	– Höhlen
rocks	– Felsen
to seal off	– abriegeln
to refuse	– sich weigern
to object	– Einwände haben

stop you. However, there is one thing we must insist on: There must be nothing published without permission from us beforehand."

The journalist returned the officer's smile. "It's a rather unwelcome condition, but I think it's justified in this case. I agree."

"Good. Then I'll let you know tomorrow what we've decided to do."

It was hardly twenty-four hours later that Inspector Kemal and Joanna Minetti met again.

"We've been thinking things over very carefully," the Inspector began, "and we thought it would be better if you were my wife."

Joanna was so surprised that she stepped back stammering "But… but… I never dreamed you'd…"

Kemal had to smile. "I'd be a lucky man to have a wife like you, Miss Minetti, but our 'marriage' is only for the purposes of next Friday's sightseeing tour. It will look more convincing if we travel as a married couple."

to insist on	– bestehen auf
to publish	– veröffentlichen
permission	– Erlaubnis
to return	– erwidern
condition	– Bedingung
to justify	– rechtfertigen
to agree	– zustimmen
to decide	– entscheiden
to stammer	– stammeln
for the purpose of	– zum Zwecke
convincing	– überzeugend
married couple	– Ehepaar

"Sorry if I reacted rather stupidly, Inspector," said the lady, smiling and blushing a bit. "It was only that the idea of finding myself suddenly with a husband seemed so preposterous... But, tell me, which of the three tourist attractions have your decided on?"

"That depends on our friend. We hope that we get him even before he reaches the place where they want to meet. At a certain point, one of our men will take over."

"But why such a roundabout way of doing things?"

"It's quite simple. We want to find out from the man bringing the forged notes where they are made. And when we know who's printing them we'll soon find out who is masterminding the operation and putting the forgeries into circulation."

"Oh, I see. But have you found out who made the call that was recorded on my type?"

"We only know that it was made here in Istanbul. But whether the caller is still in the city is another question."

"There was something else I wanted to know," said Joanna. "What did they mean by a 'package switch' and 'Number Three type packaging'?"

to react	– reagieren
preposterous	– absurd, komisch
to depend on	– abhängen von
roundabout	– umständlich
to print	– drucken
to mastermind	– lenken, leiten
to put into circulation	– in Umlauf bringen
whether	– ob

"The package switch means that there'll be two absolutely identical pieces of baggage," he explained. "At a certain spot one man arrives with such a perfectly innocent piece of luggage and when no one is looking he quickly exchanges it for the identical one with the forged notes. 'Number Three type' tells them exactly what to use: a hold-all, a sports bag, or even a guitar-case. We've no idea what they'll use until we get there."

"I understand. When do we start?"

"We'll meet up at Konya on the twenty-third, but it's a long way from Istanbul so you'd better travel up on the twenty-second, the day before, if you want to be in time for the conducted tour that starts at ten o'clock. Book yourself a room at the Hotel Sasoky. Here you are, I've written it all down for you." And Kemal handed the journalist a piece of paper.

"Thanks. So the idea is that I'll be arriving from Instanbul, but my so-called husband will be coming from Ankara?"

"Exactly. There's still a lot I have to do, so I'm going back there today. I'll collect you from the hotel on the morning of the twenty-third."

Everything went as planned. Joanna Minetti set off for Aksarai. Shortly after four in the afternoon

---

innocent	– unauffällig
to exchange	– austauschen
holdall	– Reisetasche
in time	– rechtzeitig
to book	– vorbestellen, buchen
to collect	– hier: abholen

on the twenty-second she arrived at Konya, where she parked her car in a garage and took a taxi to the Hotel Sasoky.

The room was sparsely furnished. There was a bed, a three-legged stool, a washbasin and two coat-hangers. But the view from the window was all the more beautiful by contrast. Over a distance of forty kilometres she could see clearly the peak of Mount Hassan, three thousand metres high, at the foot of which tomorrow's meeting should take place.

Next morning, towards nine o'clock, Joanna Minetti was already waiting outside the hotel when she saw Inspector Kemal coming down the street to meet her. He showed her to his car which was parked near by.

Kemal was a good driver, and as they travelled towards Aksarai he told his companion that he had twenty-four men standing by to make sure they would bring it off.

At twenty to ten they arrived at the large car park. From here they would have to go by bus.

Kemal scrutinized the twenty or so people standing at the bus stop but so unobtrusively that no one

---

sparsely	– dürftig, knapp
to furnish	– möblieren
stool	– Schemel
by contrast	– im Gegensatz dazu
peak	– Gipfel
to bring off	– schaffen, erfolgreich sein
to scrutinize	– sorgfältig anschauen
unobtrusively	– unaufdringlich

was aware of it. Joanna Minetti on the contrary was enthusiastically taking photographs of everything in sight.

At eight minutes to ten, the bus that ran from the car park to the archaeological sites came into view. It was painted bright red, and it had four extra headlamps. Seven passengers got off, and twelve of those waiting, not counting Kemal and Miss Minetti, took their seats. The party consisted of three men, five women and four children.

The man from Interpol and the journalist had the back seat to themselves.

"There are only three men," whispered Joanna.

"That makes things much easier for us," answered Kemal, "let's hope our man is one of them."

"One has a black briefcase, another a rucksack, and the third has only a plactic shopping-bag. You can see what's inside it. Two bananas and what looks like a bottle of water."

"You're very observant," said Kemal. "What else have you noticed?"

"That they're all travelling alone."

"Very good. Anything more?"

"That two of the men are probably Turks and the other is a foreigner. I wonder what the fellow with the rucksack is doing here? He has a rope and a

archaeological sites	– archäologische Plätze
to consist of	– bestehen aus
back seat	– hinterste Bank
briefcase	– Aktentasche
observant	– aufmerksam
rope	– Seil

pick too."

Kemal shrugged. "I'm told the Romchiko Caves are a paradise for potholers, and the Cersa Rocks are also very interesting for them. Who do you think is Dogan?"

This time it was the journalist who shrugged. "I've no idea. Each of them looks more harmless than the next. But why don't you ask them for their identity papers?"

"Because Dogan is only a cover-up. It's not a name you'll find on anyone's identity card."

"Are you sure?"

"Absolutely certain."

"Have *you* any suspicions?"

"Yes, I have," Kemal answered thoughtfully. "But we'll have to wait to see if they're confirmed."

They went on whispering for some time taking care that the three men, who were all sitting right in front, couldn't overhear what they said.

At twenty-five minutes past ten, the bus reached the terminus, which was also the weather station for the area. There were three men waiting to con-

---

pick	– Hacke
to shrug	– mit den Achseln zucken
potholer	– Höhlenforscher, -kletterer
cover-up	– Deckname
identity paper(-card)	– Personalausweis
suspicion	– Vermutung
to confirm	– bestätigen
to take care	– dafür sorgen
to overhear	– mithören
terminus	– Endstation

duct the new arrivals.

And then things began moving fast. The women and children were allowed to go sightseeing, but the three men were shown into a room at the back of the weather station, where they were kept under escort for the time being.

Five minutes later, Inspector Kemal had the first of the men brought into another room which he was using as an office. The excited Joanna Minetti sat at the back, out of the way, but listening eagerly. The man from Interpol was very friendly and polite. "Do sit down, won't you?"

The man was short and dark haired, typical of the people of the eastern part of the country. "I must protest most strongly!" he shouted angrily, thumping the table with his fist. "I shall complain. I'll go to…" He stopped, and looking sharply at Kemal, he said: "One moment. You were on the bus just now." Then his eyes turned to Miss Minetti. "And you were sitting with that young lady there…"

"Quite right," replied Kemal calmly. "I'm a police officer and I have to ask you a few questions. It's important, I'm afraid. I see from your papers that you come from Trebizond on the Black Sea."

The man nodded. "Yes, that's where I live. I'm a teacher. But I was in Ankara this morning…"

to keep under escort	– unter Bewachung halten, bewachen
for the time being	– für den Augenblick
to thump	– pochen, hämmern
to complain	– sich beschweren
Black Sea	– Schwarzes Meer

"And your name is Alad Shuklu?"

"Yes, it is. And I'm very angry about all this."

"What are you carrying in that bag?"

Shuklu's voice still sounded very hostile as he answered: "I thought you could see for yourself. Some bananas and a bottle of drinking water. No hands-grenades, dynamite or machine guns – nothing."

Kemal smiled. One could see that the man's hostility had absolutely no effect on Kemal.

"Does the name Dogan Patani mean anything to you?"

Silence. The man seemed to be thinking hard. "No, nothing. I've never heard of such a person."

"You may go back to the next room now, Mr Shuklu, but will you please remember that you must not speak to either of the other gentlemen there."

The second man, the one with the briefcase, hurried into the room gesticulating wildly and speaking so fast that Kemal could hardly understand what he was saying. "Now listen to me, my man. Before I say one word, I want to speak with my consul. Oh, I know you, monsieur. You came with us on the bus a few minutes ago."

"I regret the inconvenience, Monsieur Orelle, but I'm afraid I really have to ask some questions. You're coming from France, aren't you?"

---

hostile   – feindselig
to regret   – bedauern
inconvenience – Unannehmlichkeit

Orelle said nothing, but only looked at the ceiling. But when no one seemed to be impressed by this he said after a while: "I refuse to answer any questions... except to agree that I'm French."

| impressed | – beeindruckt |
| except | – außer, ausgenommen |

"May I have a look into your case?"

"Here it is. All you'll find are some books about your country."

Kemal smiled. "I hope you like our country."

Monsieur Orelle wiggled his ears and said in his most ironical expression: "Until today, I liked it very much. I repeat, until today."

"Why are you here this morning?"

The man hesitated as if the question puzzled him. "Do you mean which of the ruins am I interested in?"

"Yes."

"It was the Gayana Tower I particularly wanted to see."

The inspector handed the case back to the Frenchman. "One last question. Does the name Dogan Patani mean anything to you?"

"Sorry, no, it doesn't. I've never heard it before."

The third and last of the suspects was the man with the rope, the pick and the rucksack. He, too, seemed angry. He flung his rucksack on a chair and shouted: "What's all this fuss about? Why are we treated like criminals?"

Kemal seemed genuinely concerned. "I do apolo-

---

to wiggle	– wackeln mit
to hesitate	– zögern
to puzzle	– verwirren, durcheinanderbringen
suspect	– Verdächtiger
to fling (flung, flung)	– schleudern
fuss	– Aufregung, Wirbel
to treat	– behandeln
to be genuinely concerned	– echt betroffen sein
to apologize	– sich entschuldigen

44

gize if you've been handled roughly. I gave orders…"

"I think it's a disgrace that you are holding us here without any explanation!" he interrupted.

"We are looking for a certain person. Your name is Lusin Satran?"

"Right first time. You have my papers and I see you can read. Congratulations!" replied the climber sarcastically.

"And where did you want to go this morning?"

"If you've no objection, I'm going to climb the Cersa Rocks."

"You're very keen on climbing, aren't you?"

"Yes, I am!" Satran seemed to spit out the words and at the same time he stamped the floor with his boots till it creaked.

"Aren't the Romchiko Caves more interesting?" The man waved his hand. "I know them inside out!"

"Do you also know the name Dogan Patani?" The man shook his head emphatically. "No, I've never met one of them."

Inspector Kemal thanked him courteously. "That's all, Mr Satran. You may go."

Joanna Minetti had been making one or two notes

---

to handle roughly	– grob behandeln
disgrace	– Schande
to spit	– spucken
to stamp	– stampfen
boot	– Stiefel
to creak	– krachen, knarren, quietschen
courteous(ly)	– höflich

during the questioning. She got up now and went over to Kemal, frowning. "We're no wiser than before. Where does Dogan come into it?"

"Forgive me. I can't even hint at it yet. But Dogan must know already that the game is up."

The young lady looked at the inspector as if she had seen a ghost. "Do you mean he actually *is* one of those three?"

"Correct. And if you want to know who it is, come and watch the famous 'package switch' yourself."

"But which of them is it?" she persisted, her eyes wide with excitement. "The man with the rucksack, the Frenchman with the briefcase, or the teacher with the plastic bag?"

Kemal only said: "Come and see."

Which of the three men was really Dogan? Alad Shuklu, the teacher with the plastic shopping bag? Monsieur Orelle, the tourist with the briefcase? Or Lusin Satran, the climber with the rucksack?

---

to frown	– die Stirn runzeln
the game is up	– das Spiel ist aus
to persist	– unbeirrt fortfahren, weiterfragen
excitement	– Aufregung

46

5 The book thief

In two minutes from now, thought Mrs Kay to herself, I can lock the door and go home. But as she turned to go and fetch her coat, her heart stood still. For there, in the very centre of the display at the back of the shop, where she had exposed a large and beautiful volume on Ancient Greece, there was nothing but an empty space. Mrs Kay's surprise became alarm, and then indignation. Who could have taken this expensive volume, one of the most attractive books in the whole of her shop? Mrs Amanda Kay was not the kind of person to stand there dithering. Promptly she made up her mind that the best thing she could do was to go home and telephone Mr Scott, who would still be at work. For Mr Scott was not only her lodger, but also a detective, the head of the Investigation Department of the Safe-and-Sound Insurance Company.

the very centre	– mitten in
display	– Auslage
to expose	– aufstellen, ausstellen
volume	– Band, Buch
Ancient Greece	– Griechenland des Altertums
space	– Platz, Stelle
indignation	– Entrüstung
to dither	– bibbern; zaudern
lodger	– Untermieter
investigation department	– Fahndungsabteilung
insurance company	– Versicherungsgesellschaft

"Now let's get the facts straight, Mrs Kay," said Mr Scott half an hour later when he came home from the office. "What happened exactly?"

"I only unpacked the book this afternoon, and I put it out on the counter at the back of the shop where I have a display of big illustrated books, ones on art and history and that kind of thing. There were only two customers in the shop at the time: Mrs Stubbs and Mr Lang. As it happens, they are both old customers, people I've known for several years."

"Did they actually buy anything today?" Mr Scott interrupted.

Amanda Kay nodded. "Yes. Mr Lang bought some paperbacks, two detective stories, and Mrs Stubbs bought a book on astrology. I had to find it for her, because she's very short-sighted and she'd forgotten her glasses. Her sight is so bad that she couldn't even tell which coins were which in her hand. I was handing her the parcel when the telephone rang…"

Again Mr Scott interrupted. "Were either of them carrying anything big enough to carry away a book like that without being noticed?"

"Yes, both of them, now you come to mention it. Mrs Stubbs had a large shopping-bag, and Mr Lang…" Here Mrs Kay frowned and tried hard to

to get the facts straight	– Klarheit in die Fakten bringen
as it happens	– zufällig
actual	– tatsächlich
short-sighted	– kurzsichtig
coin	– Münze

remember." ...Mr Lang had a big briefcase."

"And you discovered the book was missing after they had left?"

"That's right," nodded Mrs Kay. "And they were my last customers today. No one else came in after they had gone. So it must have been either Mrs Stubbs or Mr Lang who took it."

"Which of them left the shop first?"

Again Mrs Kay had to think. "Mr Lang left first, I'm pretty sure."

"Good. Now give me their addresses and I'll go and hear what they have to say."

Mr Lang peered suspiciously as he opened his front door the merest crack. "What do you want?" he barked.

"I'd like to speak to you, Mr Lang. I've come at the request of Mrs Kay, the lady who keeps the bookshop in King Street."

Albert Lang pointed to a chair. "I suppose you'd better sit down," he said grudgingly. "Is there anything the matter with Mrs Kay?"

Mr Scott sat down and came straight to the point. "This afternoon, Mrs Kay put on display a new and extremely expensive illustrated book. The price is £ 20 and now it's disappeared. Mrs Kay said, you are a customer of many years' stand-

suspicious(ly)	– argwöhnisch
the merest crack	– einen ganz kleinen Spalt
at the request of	– auf Bitten von
grudging(ly)	– grollend
of many years' standing	– langjährig, alt

ing…"

"I am indeed," he nodded. "And this book has disappeared, you say? It wasn't by any chance that fat book on archaeological excavations, was it?"

"The very one. Do you know anything about it?" There was something in Mr Scott's voice that made Albert Lang stare at his visitor with growing disbelief. "I see," he said at last. "You've come to find out if I stole it. Of course I didn't. Mrs Kay should know me better than that. I suggest you go and see the lady who was also in the bookshop at the same time. She may know more than I do. And now I'd be much obliged if you'd go." And, very firmly, he showed Mr Scott the way out.

Mrs Stubbs gave Mr Scott a much friendlier welcome. She even offered him a glass of beer. And when he asked her what she knew, she looked at him astonished. "And do you really think I have stolen this book? My dear sir, you're very much mistaken." Her voice sank to an excited whisper. "But I noticed something when I was leaving the shop. There was a man at the far side. I was standing several metres away, and he didn't know I could see him. And this fellow was turning the pages of a thick book called *Treasures of Ancient Greece.*"

---

by any chance	– zufällig
excavation	– Ausgrabung
disbelief	– Mißtrauen
to be obliged	– zu Dank verbunden, dankbar
to be mistaken	– im Irrtum sein
treasure	– Schatz

"Hm," murmured Mr Scott. "Did you actually see him concealing the book?"

Mrs Stubbs shook her head. "No, I can't honestly say I saw him in the act, but all the same…"

"Never mind, madam. It doesn't matter. We're nearer a solution now."

The lady sighed with relief. "Then you don't suspect me any longer!"

"I'm only here to ask questions, Mrs Stubbs. That was all Mrs Kay asked me to do, but I think she will get in touch with you again if she needs to. Good night, Mrs Stubbs."

Half an hour later, Mr Scott was back at home and able to make a report to his landlady. And she in turn was very pleased that her lodger had succeeded in discovering the truth. And she made up her mind that she would go and have a serious talk with the book-thief, now that she knew who it was.

Which of the two customers had stolen the book?

---

to conceal	– heimlich einstecken
solution	– Lösung
relief	– Erleichterung
to get in touch	– sich in Verbindung setzen
landlady	– Wirtin, Vermieterin
to discover	– entdecken, finden
to succeed	– Erfolg haben
truth	– Wahrheit

6 The eyewitness

It was eleven minutes past twelve on a fine Saturday night in June. At the far end of Garden Avenue stood two houses with an old streetlamp in front of them.

There was no one about, except for old Mr Jensen, who was sitting on a bench at a dark corner of the street. He was enjoying a quiet smoke before turning in for the night. All at once he leaned forward, for someone was strolling down the street and coming in his direction.

When the person reached a big Mercedes, model 280 S, that was parked in the street, he paused, stepped closer to the car, did something to the window, opened the door and took out various articles. He then disappeared into Number Twenty-one, one of the two houses close by.

The old gentleman was immediately reassured. He knew them all at Number Twenty-one, the owner Mrs Hagen, and all her four ledgers, who were students.

He had completely forgotten what he had seen until he happened to notice a short item in Tuesday's newspaper:

about	– hier: in der Nähe
to stroll	– schlendern
various	– verschieden(e)
to reassure	– hier: beruhigen
to happen to notice	– zufällig bemerken
item	– Notiz

On Saturday evening, a valuable camera and other photographic equipment together with an irreplaceable reel of underwater photos were stolen from a car parked in Garden Avenue. Anyone who can help with informations is asked to call at any police station.

On reading this, Augustus Jensen set out for the nearby police station, and soon he was sitting in the office of Inspector Henry Herbert.

"It's like this, Inspector," he explained. "I could not see the person's face because I wasn't wearing my glasses. But I saw everything else. First the chap fiddled a bit with the window, then the door.

valuable	– wertvoll
equipment	– Ausrüstung(sgegenstände)
irreplaceable	– unersetzbar
reel	– Film
to fiddle with	– sich zu schaffen machen an,

Finally he took something out of the car and disappeared into Number Twenty-one."

"Didn't you suspect it was a thief?"

"No, of course not!" Mr Jensen was quite indignant. "If I'd thought that, I'd have come straight to the police."

"I'm sure you would, Mr Jensen," said the friendly inspector. "Now, do you think it was one of the students?"

"You mean one of Mrs Hagen's lodgers?"

"Exactly."

"Who else could it have been? Mrs Hagen won't be running round the streets at midnight, not at her age, and, in any case, I'm sure it was a man."

"Very well. I'll go round there and have a talk with the old lady."

Exactly an hour later Inspector Herbert stood face to face with Mrs Hagen. His luck was in, for he found that all four students happened to be at home. But Mrs Hagen was most distressed, and as he climbed the stairs to the first floor he left the lady in tears at the very idea that one of "her boys" could have done such a thing.

It was with Willie Hope, a physics student, that the inspector began. "I'm Inspector Herbert from the local police station. There are one or two ques-

chap	– Kerl
indignant	– entrüstet
his luck was in	– er hatte Glück
distressed	– bekümmert, besorgt
local	– örtlich

tions I'd like to ask you, Mr Hope."

William Hope looked a bit sheepish. "Have I committed a crime or something?" he asked frowning.

"That's what I want to know! On Saturday night, various things were stolen from a car parked in this street. Whoever took them disappeared into this house."

"And I'm supposed to be that chap?"

"I'm trying to find him. What were you doing last Saturday night?"

"I went to the movies. The film was over at about ten, and I came straight home to bed."

"Did anything suspicious strike you?"

"No. I didn't hear anything. What was stolen?"

Instead of answering directly, the inspector asked another question. "Do you do much photography?"

"A bit. The odd snap, you know. I'm no expert."

"May I look round your room?"

"Of course. But if you're looking for a camera, you won't find one."

Inspector Herbert looked at Willie Hope searchingly before asking: "Why does it have to be a camera I'm looking for?"

The young man shrugged his shoulders. "It's only that you were asking me about photography, so I

sheepish	– schüchtern, blöd
to commit a crime	– ein Verbrechen begehen
to strike	– hier: auffallen
odd snap	– gewöhnliches Knipsen, Alltagsphotographie
searching(ly)	– forschend

thought…"

The police officer nodded curtly and went to the door. "Many thanks for now. I may have to come back again later to see you."

The second student was Martin Singer. He was working on a radio set as the inspector entered.

"Good morning. Are you Mr Singer?"

The young man grinned. "I might be. Do you want to tell me I'm not?"

"Hardly," replied Herbert with a smile. "But I want you to tell me something else. I'm from the police and I have reason to believe there's a thief in this house."

"How exciting! And what do you think I have stolen?"

"Last Saturday evening, some photographic equipment was stolen from a parked car. The man was seen but not recognized, unfortunately. However, there is one thing an eyewitness saw: He entered this house immediately afterwards. What were you doing on Saturday night, Mr Singer?"

The student didn't need much time to think. "Several things, if I remember rightly. I wrote an essay, I replied to a few letters and I worked for a while on this radio set I'm building. And at about eleven o'clock I finally went off to bed."

"Have you any witnesses?"

curt(ly)	– knapp, kurz
reason	– Grund
to recognize	– erkennen
unfortunately	– unglücklicherweise
essay	– Abhandlung, Aufsatz

Singer shook his head. "No, but all the same I can prove that I wasn't the fellow who did it. At the time of the theft I was listening to the radio, that book programme *Midnight to 1 a.m.* to be precise."

The inspector's hand was already on the door-handle. "I see. Good. Now I'll go and try my luck with your neighbour."

The third student was called Peter Rose. He had a rather jolly bushy beard, but his manner was anything but jolly. "Why do you come to me?" he asked grudgingly.

"You haven't seen any photographic equipment in this house during the last few days?"

Peter Rose shook his head decisively, but he still looked annoyed. "Nothing like that."

"What did you do last Saturday evening?"

"I was studying. I always do in the evenings. Actually I was studying in the whole of Saturday."

"Do you know anything about cars?"

The student pulled his beard. "I know how to get in and out of a car, and that it is running with petrol," he replied sarcastically. "Oh yes. I know it has to be licensed, and that's quite expensive."

all the same	– trotzdem
to prove	– beweisen
theft	– Diebstahl
to be precise	– um es genau zu sagen
a jolly bushy beard	– einen lustigen buschigen Bart
manner	– Betragen, Verhalten
annoyed	– verärgert
petrol	– Benzin
it has to be licensed	– es muß zugelassen werden

"The equipment I mentioned was stolen from a four-door Mercedes car. You didn't go for a walk on Saturday night, did you?"

"I really can't remember. Honestly, Inspector, I haven't the slightest recollection."

The inspector smiled and went out. "Oh well. Perhaps the gentleman next door knows a little more."

Sebastian Kaufmann, the fourth lodger, was closing a suitcase as the inspector entered. "Are you going away?" he asked.

"What business is that of yours? Who are you anyway?"

The inspector bowed ironically. "My friends call me Henry. Some of my acquaintances, shall we say, call me Handcuffs Harry. Otherwise, Inspector Henry Herbert. Satisfied?"

The young man nodded and blushed. "Thank you, Inspector. What can I do for you?"

"Did you leave the house on Saturday evening?"

"Last Saturday evening? Let me think. Yes, I did. I was out between eleven o'clock and midnight."

"Think again, Mr Kaufmann. Wasn't it a little later than that?"

"Not really. I'd been back over a quarter of an hour when someone else came in – at exactly twenty past twelve. I happened to look at my watch."

---

recollection	– Erinnerung
to bow	– sich verbeugen
handcuffs	– Handschellen

"And who was it?"

"I've no idea."

"How do you know the time so precisely?"

"I've just told you. I looked at my watch as the front door slammed."

Inspector Herbert pointed to two empty cases. "Are you going away for long?"

Kaufmann hesitated. "I'm not going away on holiday, if that's what you think," he said at last, reaching for one of the empty cases. "But before your conclusions are going the wrong direction, let me explain that I'm moving. Oh, it's not because anything's been stolen... It's personal. If you must know, I've had a row with someone here. And now may I finish my packing, or do you object?"

"Do go on with your packing, Mr Kaufmann. I haven't the slightest objection."

Mrs Hagen was waiting for the inspector downstairs. "Have you seen them all, Inspector? None of them could have done a thing like that, I'm sure. It's all been a mistake, hasn't it?"

The Inspector felt rather awkward, but he had to tell the lady the truth. "I'm sorry to disappoint you, Mrs Hagen, but one of your students is in fact the thief..."

Which of the four students was the thief?

---

to slam	– (Tür) knallen
to move	– umziehen (in ein anderes Zimmer/Haus)
row	– Streit, Auseinandersetzung
awkward	– hier: in einer unangenehmen Lage, verlegen

7 A shocking talk

That Friday morning, Mrs Bloom was in a greater hurry than ever to get her housework done. The reason for such haste was that she had an appointment at her dressmaker's, and Mrs Lutter was always very upset if her customers were late. Mrs Bloom had to be there at ten o'clock, so she tidied and dusted and polished as if she were trying to set a new world record.

At half past nine she had finished. Pleased with herself, she went through the gleaming rooms of her flat and got herself ready to go out. Then she put on her coat, placed her handbag ready on the table and went to the telephone to order a taxi.

Mrs Bloom lifted the receiver to her ear and her right forefinger was about to dial the number when she hesitated. No doubt, there was a man's voice on the phone. Puzzled, she was about to replace the receiver and start again when she heard a second voice. This voice, too, could only have been a man's and Mrs Bloom turned white. She held the doorpost and her knees began to tremble. What

---

appointment	– Verabredung, Termin
dressmaker	– Schneider(in)
upset	– ungehalten
to gleam	– funkeln, strahlen
to dial	– wählen
to hesitate	– zögern

she heard was so awful, so dreadful…

"…I wasn't born yesterday, Tony. I've been watching the place all week."

"Sunday too, Ginger?"

"Sure, Sunday too. But that wouldn't be any good. Too many people about. Monday would be the best day."

"OK then. Let's do it on Monday. Have you got it all worked out?"

"I'll say I have! We'll go to the last one, Tony, and when it's finished we'll hide until everyone else has gone. When the little blonde with the ice-cream has fetched her coat and left, there'll only be the boss sitting at the till, counting all that lovely money. He's always the last to go."

"And how will we get out?"

"As soon as we've made it clear to the boss that we need Monday's takings more than he does, we'll tie him up politely but efficiently in his chair, and we'll make our get-away through one of the emergency exits. Ha! Ha!"

"Damn it all, Ginger. The poor fellow'll have to spend all night tied up in that little cubbyhole. Do you think he'll be all right?"

---

dreadful	= awful
till	– Kasse
takings	– Einnahmen
efficiently	– wirkungsvoll
to tie up	– festbinden
to make the get-away	– abhauen
emergency exit	– Notausgang
cubbyhole	– Raum, „Kabuff"

"Don't worry, Tony. The cleaner will find him early on Tuesday morning. Besides, they always come to change the pictures in the display cases on Tuesday mornings. Everything clear?"

___

display case   – Schaukasten

"Yeah, perfectly clear. We'll meet as usual, in front of the big poster."

With shaking hands, Mrs Bloom carefully replaced the receiver and dropped into an armchair. Five minutes and a glass of brandy later, she felt strong enough to ring the police, but her hands were still trembling...

On Monday evening, both Tony and Ginger were also trembling... but with rage. The police were waiting for them...

What kind of place had the two villains tried to rob?

---

to replace — auflegen; ersetzen
villain — Schurke

8 The jazz trumpet

Late one Saturday night there was a break-in at Christiansen & Sons, a big musical instrument shop in Copenhagen. The investigations that followed made it perfectly clear that this was not the work of a gang, but of a single person.

The culprit had smashed the glass pane of a side door in a dark yard, which was normally used only as a staff entrance. He had broken up three cash registers, and had taken 1,225 Kroner from them. Then he had stolen the most valuable instrument from the shop window display, a golden jazz trumpet worth 14,000 Kroner. He had replaced it in the window by an ordinary trumpet, but had used its case to carry away the stolen instrument. The police was sure that the burglar must have worn gloves, as there were no fingerprints anywhere.

These were the facts of the case. Only twelve hours later however the police found unmistakable evidence that the thief could only have been someone employed at the grocery warehouse next door. For

break-in	– Einbruch
to smash	– zerschlagen
pane	– Scheibe
krone, kroner	– dänische Krone, Kronen
ordinary	– gewöhnlich, normal
fingerprint	– Fingerabdruck
unmistakable evidence	– klare Beweise
to employ	– beschäftigen

there, on the third floor, when the building was searched, was found a big box. And hidden in the box were the stolen trumpet and 1,200 Kroner. The rest of 25 Kroner was missing.

After interrogating all the warehouse staff on Monday morning, the officer was able to eliminate everyone except the firm's three junior trainees. One of them must have done it.

So they were brought before Mr Sorensen, the Chairman of the Juvenile Court. But when they had expected that Mr Sorensen would start asking a lot of questions they were very much mistaken. Instead he handed them pencils and paper and told them to sit down at different tables as if to write a test! And their eyes grew wider still when Mr Sorensen began to speak.

"I've sent for you so that I can find out which of you is the thief," he began in a firm but friendly voice. "Yes, I'm quite certain that one of you is guilty. You all insist you know nothing about the break-in, nothing about the theft of the trumpet, and nothing about the missing money. Well, you may say so and until we can prove the contrary we

---

grocery warehouse	– Lebensmittellagerhaus, Großmarkt
to interrogate	– verhören
to eliminate	– ausschließen
trainee	– Lehrling, Auszubildender
Chairman of the Juvenile Court	– Vorsitzende des Jugendgerichts
guilty	– schuldig
to insist	– bestehen auf; beharren
to prove the contrary	– das Gegenteil beweisen

must believe you. All the same, I'm an inquisitive person, and there's something I'd like to know." Here he paused for a moment, and then went on more slowly: "What I wonder is how a completely innocent young man would tell such a story. How does he think it happened? So, I've given you each paper and pencil and I'm allowing you half an hour to write me a short composition about this theft from the music shop. Imagine you are the burglar. Put yourself in his place. Describe how you got in, what you stole, and how you covered up your traces. Is that clear? Very good. Remember that you have thirty minutes starting now. And don't forget to put your name at the top of the paper!"

Mr Sorensen looked on his watch, sat down, pulled a newspaper from his pocket and began reading it. Or rather, he only pretended to read. From the corner of his eye he was in fact watching every movement of the three boys, who all hesitated for some time, and then began writing reluctantly, as if they mistrusted the whole business.

Exactly half an hour later Mr Sorensen told the boys to stop writing and to bring him their compositions. This is what he read:

Jan Hansen: I broke into the music shop. I'd al-

inquisitive	– neugierig
composition	– Aufsatz
to imagine	– sich vorstellen
to cover up	– verwischen
trace	– Spur
reluctantly	– widerwillig
to mistrust the business	– der Sache mißtrauen

ready had a good look round in the morning to see where I could get in. The yard seemed the best place. There aren't any lights there. So I smashed a window and got in easily. Then I looked for some money. I found some and put it in my pocket. When I'd got enough, I took an expensive trumpet from the window. I moved very quietly so that no one could hear me. I took off my shoes and carried them in my hand. It was very dark, and I had to look out so I didn't fall over things. As soon as I had the money and the trumpet I crept out again.

Carsten Laag: If I wanted to break into the music shop, I'd cut a big hole in the window with a glass cutter. As no one would know it was me, I should not put on gloves. I could put the trumpet in a case and hide it under my coat. I shouldn't touch the three cash registers. They'd make too much noise. I would also take some records, because they're easy to sell.

Arne Hendriksen: I broke into the music shop during the night. I got in by the side door, because it wouldn't be noticed there. And it's very dark there as well. I wore gloves so I wouldn't leave any fingerprints. First I collected the money from various drawers, and then I took the trumpet out of the window. It's a wonderful instrument, and I'd always wanted it. With the money I found I'll buy myself some real warm leather gloves. I'll wait to sell the trumpet till people have forgotten all about it, and then no one will suspect it's been stolen.

Mr Sorensen looked up. "Yes, I thought so. Two of you may go, but you and I, my lad" – and here he picked out one of them – "are going to have a little talk by ourselves. And you're going to tell me exactly why you went shop-breaking…"

Which of the three junior trainees had given himself away?

---

drawer	– Schublade
leather gloves	– Lederhandschuhe
to suspect	– vermuten
to give away	– sich verraten

Solutions

The face at the window, page 7
Frank Daimler said that he had never received his uncle's letter. If that were true, he couldn't have known the name of the "face at the window". But he said "The police ought to arrest this fellow Walters…" before Paul Daimler had actually mentioned the man's name.

The fare-dodger, page 17
The real fare-dodger was the man in seat seventy-three. He told the others he had "only got in at Doorn", but the train hadn't stopped there. We are clearly told that "the train rushed on through Doorn station".

Find the mistakes, page 22
There are seven mistakes of fact in this story:
1   Only one of the two men whose portraits were hanging in the hall was American. Charles Dickens was English;
2   Charles Dickens, the novelist, was never President of the USA;
3   Abraham Lincoln was President of the United States of America, but hardly a well-known novelist;
4   At first the party was said to be for Sir Arthur's fiftieth birthday. Later it was said to be in honour of his appointment as a minister;
5   Mulligan brought three officers with him at first, but later he put four men on duty;
6   The "anonymous telephone call" about the pickpocket became an "anonymous letter" later on;
7   The conjurer collected twelve watches, but only eleven gentlemen checked their pockets afterwards.

A case for Interpol, page 27

The wanted man was Lusin Satran because he was the only one who knew that Dogan Patani was not the name of one man but the names of two different people. Besides, he could be detected from the start because of what he was carrying. A plastic bag was quite unsuitable, and a briefcase too obvious. Only the rucksack would have served the purpose.

The book thief, page 47

It was Mrs Stubbs who was the thief. How could she have seen the title of a book from a distance of several metres when she was particularly short-sighted and had forgotten her glasses?

The eyewitness, page 53

The thief was the student named Martin Singer. He betrayed himself saying: "At the time of the theft I was listening to the radio, that book programme *Midnight to 1 a.m...*." Only the eyewitness and one other person could have known that the theft took place within this period of time. And that one person was the thief.

A shocking talk, page 61

The place they intended to rob could only have been a cinema.

The jazz trumpet, page 65

The culprit was Carsten Laag. He gave himself away by writing that the trumpet was carried away in a case, and that he knew there were three cash registers in the shop. Besides, it was very silly of him to write in the essay almost the exact opposite of what had actually happened.

to mention	– erwähnen
to put on duty	– auf Posten schicken
obvious	– auffällig
to serve the purpose	– dem Zweck dienen
to betray oneself	– sich verraten

Vocabulary

to take ~	– in ~ treten
to admit [əd'mit]	– zugeben, bestätigen
ancient ['einʃənt]	– alt, aus dem Altertum
to annoy [ə'nɔi]	– verärgern
answering machine ['ɑːnsriŋ mə'ʃiːn]	– (Telefon-) Beantworter
to apologize [ə'pɔlədʒaiz]	– sich entschuldigen
appointment [ə'pɔintmənt]	– Ernennung
archaeological [ɑːkiə'lɔdʒikl]	– archäologisch
arrival [ə'raivəl]	– Ankömmling, Ankunft
atmospherics [ætməs'feriks]	– atmosphärische Störungen
awkward ['ɔːkwəd]	– unwohl, verlegen
B back seat ['bæksiːt]	– hintere Bank
to behave [bi'heiv]	– sich benehmen, verhalten
to betray [bi'trei]	– sich verraten
to blaze into light [bleiz]	– hell aufleuchten
to blush [blʌʃ]	– erröten
to book [buk]	– buchen, vorbestellen
boot [buːt]	– Stiefel
to bow [bau]	– sich verbeugen
brains [breinz]	– führende Köpfe
breath [breθ]	– Atem
breathing ['briːðiŋ]	– Atmen
briefcase ['briːfkeis]	– Aktentasche
to bring off [briŋ-'ɔːf]	– schaffen, erfolgreich sein
burst [bəːst]	– Ausbruch, Schwall
C calm(ly) [kɑːm]	– ruhig
canvas ['kænvəs]	– Leinwand
(to take) care [kɛə]	– dafür sorgen
caves [keivz]	– Höhlen

to celebrate ['selibreit]	– feiern
in the very centre ['sentə]	– mitten in
by any chance [tʃɑːns]	– zufällig
chandelier [ʃændi'liə]	– Kronleuchter
chap [tʃæp]	– Kerl
to check [tʃek]	– überprüfen
circulation [səːkju'leiʃn]	– Umlauf
coach [kəutʃ]	– Wagen, Waggon
coincidence [kəu'insidəns]	– Zufall, Zusammentreffen
to collect [kə'lekt]	– hier: abholen
to commit [kə'mit]	– hier: begehen, verüben
compartment [kəm'pɑːtmənt]	– Abteil
to complain [kəm'plein]	– sich beschweren
to conceal [kən'siːl]	– heimlich einstecken, verheimlichen
to be concerned [kən'səːnd]	– betroffen sein
condition [kən'diʃn]	– Bedingung
conducted [kən'dʌktid]	– mit Führung, Reiseleitung
to confine [kən'fain]	– beschränken
to confirm [kən'fəːm]	– bestätigen
conjurer ['kʌndʒərə]	– Zauberer
consignment [kən'sainmənt]	– Lieferung
to consist (of) [kən'sist]	– bestehen aus
contempt [kən'tempt]	– Verachtung
by contrast ['ɔntrast]	– im Vergleich mit, im Gegensatz
convincing [kən'vinsiŋ]	– überzeugend
to cover ['kʌvə]	– bedecken
cover-up ['kʌvə'r-ʌp]	– Deckname
(married) couple [kʌpl]	– Ehepaar
courteous(ly) ['kəːtjəs]	– höflich
crack [kræk]	– Spalt
to creek [kriːk]	– krachen, knarren, quietschen

crime [kraim]	– Verbrechen
curt(ly) [kə:t]	– kurz, knapp
D to decide [di'said]	– entscheiden
to deliver [di'livə]	– übergeben
to deny [di'nai]	– zurückweisen, verneinen
to depend on [di'pend]	– abhängen von
to dial ['daiəl]	– wählen
disapproval [disə'pru:vəl]	– Mißbilligung
disbelief ['disbili:f]	– Mißtrauen
to discover [dis'kʌvə]	– entdecken, finden
disgrace [dis'greis]	– Schande
disguise [dis'gaiz]	– Verkleidung
display [dis'plei]	– Auslage
distressed [dis'trest]	– bekümmert, besorgt
to dither ['diðə]	– bibbern, zaudern
duty ['dju:ti]	– Pflicht, Aufgabe; Posten, Wache
E eery ['iəri]	– unheimlich
eight-piece orchestra	– Acht-Mann-Orchester
emphatical [im'fætikəl]	– voller Überzeugung
to ensure [in'ʃuə]	– sicherstellen
entertainment [entə'teinmənt]	– Unterhaltung
entrance hall ['entrəns]	– Eingangshalle
(to keep under) escort ['eskɔ:t]	– bewachen
equipment [i'kwipmənt]	– Gerät, Ausrüstung
essay ['esei]	– Abhandlung, Aufsatz
except [ik'sept]	– außer, ausgenommen
excitement [ig'saitmənt]	– Aufregung, Erregung
to expose [iks'pəuz]	– aufstellen, ausstellen
F fate [feit]	– Schicksal
to fiddle with ['fidl wið]	– sich zu schaffen machen an
to fit	– passen zu
to fit in	– hineinpassen
to fix	– anschließen

to flicker ['flikə]	– flackern
to fling, flung[ʌ]flung[ʌ]	– schleudern
forged [fɔːdʒd]	– gefälscht
to frown [fraun]	– die Stirne runzeln
to furnish ['fəːniʃ]	– möblieren
further ['fəːðə]	– weitere
furtive(ly) ['fəːtiv]	– verstohlen
fuss [fʌs]	– Aufregung, Wirbel
G the game [geim] is up	– das Spiel ist aus
genuine(ly) ['dʒenjuin]	– echt
gesticulate [dʒes'tikjuleit]	– gestikulieren, (herum)fuchteln
glove [glʌv]	– Handschuh
government ['gʌvənmənt]	– Regierung
graceful(ly) ['greisful]	– graziös
to grind [graind]	– knirschen
grudging(ly) ['grʌdʒiŋ]	– grollend
guard [gɑːd]	– Schaffner
H handcuff ['hændkʌf]	– Handschelle
to handle [hændl]	– behandeln
to happen to…	– zufällig…
to haunt [hɔːnt]	– verfolgen
health [helθ]	– Gesundheit
to hesitate ['heziteit]	– zögern
historic ruins	– historische Ruinen
holdall ['həuldɔːl]	– Reisetasche
host [həust]	– Gastgeber
hostile ['hɔstail]	– feindselig
hostility [hɔs'tiliti]	– Feindseligkeit
I identical [ai'dentikəl]	– gleich aussehend
identity paper (~ card) [ai'dentiti]	– Personalausweis
imagination [imædʒi'neiʃn]	– Fantasie, Vorstellungskraft
impressed [im'prest]	– beeindruckt
to include [in'kluːd]	– einschließen, einbeziehen

inconspicuous [inkən'spikjuəs]	–	unauffällig
inconvenience [inkən'viːnjəns]	–	Unannehmlichkeit
independent [indi'pendənt]	–	unabhängig
indignant [in'dignənt]	–	entrüstet, empört
indignation [indig'neiʃən]	–	Entrüstung
innocent ['inəsənt]	–	unschuldig, unauffällig
inscribed [in'skraibd]	–	mit der Aufschrift versehen
insist on [in'sist]	–	bestehen auf
insurance [in'ʃuərəns]	–	Versicherung
to introduce oneself ['intrədjuːs]	–	sich vorstellen, bekanntmachen
investigation [investi'geiʃn]	–	Untersuchung, Fahndung
irreplaceable [irə'pleisəbl]	–	unersetzbar
item ['aitəm]	–	Notiz, Stück, Gegenstand
J to join in [dʒɔin]	–	sich beteiligen
to justify ['dʒʌstifai]	–	rechtfertigen
L landlady ['lænleidi]	–	Wirtin, Vermieterin
leather ['leðə]	–	Leder
to license ['laisəns]	–	zulassen
local ['loukəl]	–	örtlich
lodger ['lɔdʒə]	–	Untermieter
luck [lʌk]	–	Glück
his luck was in	–	er hatte Glück
M manner ['mænə]	–	Betragen
to mastermind ['maːstəmaind]	–	lenken, leiten
to mention [menʃn]	–	erwähnen
message ['mesidʒ]	–	Mitteilung
to make up one's mind	–	sich entschließen
to mingle ['miŋgl]	–	sich mischen (unter)
to be mistaken [mis'teikən]	–	im Irrtum sein
moustache [məs'taːʃ]	–	Schnurrbart
murmur ['məːmə]	–	Murmeln
N nasty ['naːsti]	–	unangenehm

novelist ['nɔvəlist]	–	(Roman-)Schriftsteller
O to object [əb'dʒekt]	–	Einwände haben
to be obliged [əb'laidʒd]	–	verpflichtet sein; zu Dank verbunden, dankbar sein
observant [ɔb'zə:vənt]	–	aufmerksam
obvious ['ɔbviəs]		hier: auffällig
odd snap ['ɔd 'snæp]	–	Gelegenheitsfoto
oil painting ['ɔil 'peintiŋ]	–	Ölgemälde
ominous ['ɔminəs]	–	unheilvoll
to operate ['ɔpəreit]	–	Geschäfte abwickeln, tätig werden
to overhear [əuvə'hiə]	–	mithören
P package switch ['pækidʒ 'switʃ]	–	Gepäcktausch
particular(ly) [pə'tikjulə]	–	besonders
to pat [pæt]	–	klopfen
peak [pi:k]	–	Gipfel
to peer [piə]	–	gucken
permission [pə'miʃən]	–	Erlaubnis
to persist [pə'sist]	–	unbeirrt fortfahren, weiterfragen
to persuade [pə'sueid]	–	überreden
petrol ['petrəl]	–	Benzin
pick [pik]	–	Hacke, Pickel
pickpocket ['pikpɔkit]	–	Taschendieb
to pick up [pik'ʌp]	–	erwischen, schnappen
pie; finger in the ~	–	Pastete; die Hand im Spiel
plain clothes [kləuðiz]	–	Zivil(Kleidung)
playback key [ki:]	–	Wiedergabetaste
pleasure ['pleʒə]	–	Vergnügen
politely [pə'laitli]	–	höflich
in position [pə'ziʃn]	–	an Ort und Stelle
potholer ['pɔthəulə]	–	Höhlenforscher, -kletterer
preposterous [pri'pɔstərəs]	–	absurd, komisch

to print [print]	– drucken
to prove [pru:v]	– beweisen
to publish ['pʌbliʃ]	– veröffentlichen
punch [pʌntʃ]	– Schlag, Stoß
purpose for the ~ of ['pə:pəs]	– zum Zwecke
to puzzle [pʌzl]	– verwirren
R to raise [reiz]	– erheben
reason ['ri:zn]	– Grund
to reassure [riə'ʃuə]	– beruhigen, versichern
receiver [ri'si:və]	– Telefonhörer
to reckon ['rekən]	– schätzen, rechnen
to recognize ['rekəgnaiz]	– erkennen
recollection [rekə'lekʃən]	– Erinnerung
to record [ri'kɔ:d]	– aufzeichnen, aufnehmen
reel [ri:l]	– Film
to refuse [ri'fju:z]	– sich weigern
to regret [ri'gret]	– bedauern
relief [ri'li:f]	– Erleichterung
to relieve [ri'li:v]	– erleichtern
to rely [ri'lai]	– sich verlassen (auf)
remark [ri'mɑ:k]	– Bemerkung
remarkable [ri'mɑ:kəbl]	– bemerkenswert
required [ri'kwaiə]	– benötigt
to resign [ri'zain]	– resignieren, aufgeben
to return [ri'tə:n]	– zurückgeben, erwidern
ring (riŋ]	– hier: Beiklang
rock	– Fels
rough(ly) [rʌf]	– grob, derb
roundabout ['raundəbaut]	– umständlich
rope [rəup]	– Seil
row [rau]	– Streit, Krach, Auseinandersetzung
rug [rʌg]	– Brücke (Teppich)
to run away with [rʌn]	– durchgehen (Fantasie usw.)

S

to scrutinize ['skru:tinaiz]	– sorgfältig anschauen
to seal off [si:l]	– abriegeln
search [sə:tʃ]	– forschen, suchen
to serve [sə:v]	– dienen
sheepish ['ʃi:piʃ]	– blöd, schüchtern
short-sighted ['ʃɔ:t'saitid]	– kurzsichtig
to shrug (ʃrʌg]	– mit den Achseln zucken
silence ['sailəns]	– Schweigen
to slam [slæm]	– (die Tür) knallen
snoring [snɔ:riŋ]	– Schnarchen
solution [səl'ju:ʃn]	– Lösung
none too soon [su:n]	– keinen Augenblick zu früh
sound(ly) [saund]	– hier: tief
sparce(ly) ['spɛəs(li)]	– dürftig, knapp
speech [spi:tʃ]	– Rede
to spit [spit]	– spucken
to stammer ['stæmə]	– stammeln
to stamp [stæmp]	– stampfen
standing (of many years ~)	– langjährig, alt
stool [stu:l]	– Schemel
straight ahead [streit]	– geradeaus
to get straight [streit]	– Klarheit bringen in
to strike [straik]	– hier: auffallen
to stroll [strəul]	– schlendern
stuff [stʌf]	– Stoff; hier: Falschgeld
success [sək'ses]	– Erfolg
to succeed [sək'si:d]	– Erfolg haben
to suffer ['sʌfə]	– leiden unter
superstitious [sju:pə'stiʃəs]	– abergläubisch
surprise [sə'praiz]	– Erstaunen
suspect to ~ [səs'pekt]	– verdächtigen, den Verdacht haben
suspicion [səs'piʃn]	– Verdächtigung
to switch [switʃ]	– austauschen, übergeben

	to switch to	– hier: hinüberrutschen, wechseln
T	to tackle [tækl]	– schaffen, fertig werden mit
	to take notice [teik 'noutis]	– Notiz nehmen
	tanned [tænd]	– gebräunt
	to tap [tæp]	– klopfen
	tape recorder ['teip ri'kɔːdə]	– Tonbandgerät
	tavern ['tævən]	– Taverne, Schenke
	terminus ['təːminəs]	– Endstation
	theft [θeft]	– Diebstahl
	thunderous ['θʌndərəs]	– donnernd
	to thump [θʌmp]	– pochen, hämmern
	in time [taim]	– rechtzeitig
	to tip someone off	– jemandem einen Tip geben, warnen
	top hat ['top hæt]	– Zylinder
	touch of coolness [tʌtʃ]	– ein wenig Kühle
	to get in touch [tʌtʃ]	– sich in Verbindung setzen
	track [træk]	– Strecke
	treasure ['treʒə]	– Schatz
	truth [truːθ]	– Wahrheit
	to turn up [təːn ʌp]	– auftauchen, erscheinen
U	undisturbed ['ʌndis'təːbd]	– ungestört
	unfortunately [ʌn'fɔːtʃnit]	– unglücklicherweise
	unobtrusive(ly) ['ʌnəb'truːsiv]	– unaufdringlich
	unpleasant [ʌn'plezənt]	– unangenehm
V	valuable ['væljuəbl]	– wertvoll
	various ['vɛəriəs]	– verschieden(e)
	volume ['vɔljuːm]	– Band, Buch
W	whether ['weðə]	– ob
	to wiggle [wigl]	– wackeln mit